Confidence

Unleash your inner power

By
KARIM A

Contents

Introduction

The central issue when addressing the development of self-confidence in an individual who has long believed that his self-worth is inadequate is how to get self-confidence.

Individuals with a strong sense of self can bear themselves better than those with a weak sense of self. They are the achievers, the center of society, and the people in the spotlight. They walk straight, speak clearly, and have a subtle and obvious influence on others. In short, they are those who care, and they can be seen from afar.

Self-assured people are sometimes adored by society. However, there are those self-assured people who, simply by leaving, make the room lighter.

These are two very different displays of self-assurance. One undermines a person's credibility, while the other enhances his personality. And you do not want the consequences of being overconfident in yourself, which is that people no longer see you as effective, but rather as an annoyance in their daily lives.

Self-assurance comes from within. Outside stimulation can be beneficial, but knowing yourself and applying that knowledge to gain confidence is the key to gaining self-confidence, you must understand that your limitations must not limit you and your characteristics must not destroy you. Instead, use all of these factors to create a personality that will benefit you and those around you.

"Know thyself!" exclaims Delphi's Oracle. Though this was said thousands of years ago, it is undeniably true that the wisdom it contains is still applicable today.

Learn about yourself and gain confidence. Recognize, however, that knowledge comes from within you. As a result, you must accept the fact that unless you

If you don't accept your flaws and imperfections, the demons of low self-esteem will haunt you forever.

Knowing too much about yourself can be dangerous if your self-control foundations are not well developed.

You would be exposed to your flaws, and because you do not yet have control, you may be eaten by your flaws. This condition is closely related to thought rumination, in which you appear to go around in a circle of thoughts about your losses and failures regardless of your accomplishments.

Another risk of losing control of yourself while attempting to gain self-confidence is that you may become overconfident and lose sight of the true value of having a sense of self. As previously stated, overconfidence is just as dangerous as a lack of confidence. This would return you to failures or, worse, to eventual failure.

Knowing yourself is one factor that can be either dangerous or beneficial.

Self-awareness frequently assists people in realizing how wonderful their creation was. They learn to value their abilities and characteristics, which are as unique as those of others. We are indeed all unique. Our distinguishing characteristics can be seen by closely examining our abilities and limitations. Our individuality is manifested in the natural gifts that contribute to our greater self-worth. Our uniqueness can be seen in our potential, which we can choose to ignore or maximize at will.

All of these truths would remain hidden from you unless you learned to contemplate your being and become aware of who you truly are.

Chapter 1: A Step Towards Increasing Your Self-Confidence

Everything must begin somewhere. You will be tormented indefinitely by the very thing you are afraid of unless you begin to rebuild your self-confidence.

Our self-esteem is the sum of all our reactions to life's experiences, how we were guided by older people in our environment, and how we and society perceive us.

Many factors influence our perception of confidence.

One determining factor is how well we expect ourselves and our circumstances to be. Many people fall into the trap of setting unrealistic goals. Their losses are becoming so painful that they eventually suffer the consequences of lower self-confidence.

Others, on the other hand, prefer to play it safe and set more achievable goals that are easier to achieve. And because accomplishments contribute significantly to the development of self-confidence, these people benefit from knowing that they are capable of doing something.

You've probably heard the expression "it's all in your head." And when it comes to many psychological and emotional conditions, we can say that it's all in the mind. Because they are rooted in and develop from the mind, the antidote may also come from the same source.

You can always condition yourself to feel the way you want or don't want to feel.
You can suppress emotions while also assisting them to materialize. Assume you want to hate yourself for not being good enough. If you force yourself to believe in that hatred and truly believe that you are not good enough, you will only get two results: genuine hatred and lower self-esteem.
The majority of us are completely unaware of what we are saying. We sometimes fail to check ourselves for the things we are subconsciously registering.

You may not have said it recently, but if you're used to hearing yourself mumble, "I'm a loser," or "I'm not worthy of anything," your subconscious mind may believe these are the facts.

Even as we speak, many people believe these statements.

They aren't just words. They are real, and they will delve deep into your subconscious mind to integrate them into your being. If you believe in these, you will undoubtedly believe in their polar opposite.

Belief in oneself is essential for developing self-confidence. Whatever you decide to believe will be accepted as fact. As a result, all you have to do is manipulate the values you want to acquire. Otherwise, no amount of waiting will make you change your mind. You must be the source of motivation.

Suggestions may come from outside sources, but in the end, you and only you will fight the battle.

Change must start with you. You can begin by talking to yourself in positive terms, such as "you are great" (because you truly are a great individual waiting for your talents to be discovered). Or "you are lovely" (because, believe it or not, each of us was created beautifully to bring glory to our Creator).

You can't stay mad for long about your lack of self-confidence.

You must change your outlook and live a different life that looks forward to better things.

Chapter 2: A Self-Confidence Philosophy

Everyone takes pride in all of their possessions. Whether it was our past achievements or the current way of life, each of us has become an achiever in our own right.

However, many of us may have denied this truth. But, as you can see, it is self-evident: everyone is capable of accomplishing anything if we put our hearts and minds into it. Nobody is deprived of the ability to enjoy life's triumphs. Only those who deny themselves these blessings suffer. Are you one of them?

Leave your response hanging before whispering it to yourself. Whatever the outcome is, make certain that it is for the better.

If you can say you're confident enough, that's great! But don't be satisfied with "enough." There will always be gaps, and you should take advantage of them.

If you answered no, don't waste time. Wasting your life on meaningless whimpers of negativism would cause you to regret everything every time you leave.

How painful it would be to know that you had everything you needed to succeed but chose not to use it.

There was once a young eagle who was raised in a chicken village. He was raised to believe that he is a chicken and that he lives among them.

He had been watching the eagles hover in midair with their display of magnificence for a long time.

He wishes he was born like these airborne eagles every time he stands in awe of them. He dared not spread his wings, even though his heart yearns to soar to the heights that eagles soar. He failed to realize his true potential and died as a chicken, yearning to become one of those to whom he truly belongs.

Each of us is an eagle. We are all capable of flying to our full potential.

Unless we spread our wings and dare to discover our true selves, we will be bound by our inability to reach new heights and become the people we were meant to be.

Now, if we could only recognize the eagle that is sleeping within us, we could have all lived happy and contented lives.

We were all born with the right to achieve and succeed. The Universe is so kind to us that she took the time to make sure we had everything we needed to fly. Don't squander this opportunity by carrying loads that will make you limited and thus unable to fly.

Be like an eagle that has risen from the mud of being a chicken. Chickens are raised to be slaughtered. Similarly, if we choose to be chickens, we must accept the reality that our goal will be defeated. That is, to give thanks to the Universe for keeping us in her arms and providing us with everything we needed.

Be an eagle and live a life free of the chickens' destructive culture. Be like an eagle and benefit from the confidence that comes with being a powerful creature.

Chapter 3: Building Self-Esteem and confidence

Optimism! It all boils down to our positive perception of ourselves, our surroundings, and life itself. We are bound to enjoy life the way every man should as long as we believe in the goodness that we may have.

Unfortunately, many of us are incapable of grasping optimism amid misery, morbidity, and struggles. Of course, life's pleasures would be unappreciated if they were not accompanied by unhappiness. If all we know is joy, we cannot feel pain. If we were always happy, tears would lose their value.

Confidence would not be recognized if we did not occasionally fall flat on our faces.

Life is a wonderful gift from which we can make whatever we want.

We must begin early in laying our foundations so that we do not waste precious moments that will never come again. A moment is gone forever, but your light will continue to shine long after you are gone.

We would be able to recognize the full extent of our potential if we were optimistic in life. Everyone has an equal opportunity for recognition, but many of us miss out because we surrender before the battle even begins.

You must be brave if you want to share what the world has to offer.

Nothing, not even the miserable demons of low self-confidence, should keep you from living your life.

Those who brave life are those who believe in themselves.

Sometimes we just have to take chances to find out what lies ahead. Taking risks, on the other hand, necessitates a high level of self-confidence. You'd be like a warrior without his armor if you didn't have this.

We were born with all of the abilities that we will need later in life. One such skill is the ability to face challenges with faith, both in ourselves and in Him who created us all.

Even when it appears that our neighbor is far more fortunate than us, we all had an equal opportunity to develop our sense of self.

We commonly believe that life is unfair when, in fact, it is not. We all have our fair share of blessings and challenges. It all comes down to how we perceive things and how we deal with them.

The same is true for self-esteem and confidence. Many of us believe that the man we admire shares many of life's blessings because he can bear himself better, face the public better, and is far more eloquent and confident than most of us.

Remember that before he got there, he had to overcome obstacles that boosted his self-esteem and confidence. We can all be that man if we believe in ourselves enough.

We simply need to find our enlightenment to lay solid foundations for our self-esteem and self-confidence.

Before we can accept outside help, we must first make changes within ourselves. Outside reinforcement cannot help you realize how valuable you are and how beautifully you were created if you refuse to accept this one simple truth.

Go ahead and assist in the discovery of yourself; it will be one of the most wonderful endeavors you will undertake in your life.

Chapter 4: The Roots courses of Low Self Confidence

There is no single factor that can be identified as the source of low self-confidence.

We are failing to unearth and correct the accumulation of past mistakes and deficiencies. It is the result of our inability to recognize who we truly are and what is impeding our graphs.

Low self-esteem is limiting. It would send us stomping on our endowed abilities while viewing our failures as early defeats. It would keep us in our comfort zone, where we would be safe from further humiliation and mistakes.

The comfort zones will then convince us that we must not leave their four corners because disappointments and losses await us outside.

Even if we tell ourselves how harsh and messed up things are, we must not give in to the inner critic that thrives within us. At all costs, we must defeat it and demonstrate our superiority to the rest of the world.

Low self-esteem develops during childhood. Unfortunately, many of us have parents, teachers, friends, and enemies who are more concerned with our flaws than with our strengths. They would point out our errors and kill our inner drives. These may not be said directly to our faces, but their actions and sneers are convincing enough.

Perhaps you live under cold, critical eyes that see no flaws.

Perhaps you are the underling of a successful brother, thus the intense focus on him and frequent disregard for you. People probably do things for you because they believe you are incapable of doing so on your own.

These are all subtle triggers that will contribute to your eventual loss of self-confidence.

Because of such poor models and the lack of attention paid to you, you will soon discover that you are incapable of doing things when, in fact, you possess abilities beyond your comprehension.

Your faith in their beliefs would then lead you to blame yourself for all of your failures. And you might even convince yourself that you are also responsible for the failures of those with whom you have close contact.

As a child, broad statements will be commonplace. Even without the reinforcement of the warped people around you, you will convince yourself of your stupidity.

And as the process progresses, you will learn to ignore the obvious negative accusations leveled at you by others. And, to add to your already-heavy burdens, you would come to accept that there is nothing more to live than defeats and failures.

Your self-esteem is far too low right now. As a result, you would not attempt to resolve your conflict with your sense of self, nor would you dare to plan how to avoid this self-tormenting path of life. However, solutions and helpful people would find their way to you. However, your reactions would be to either push them away or ignore them.

Continue in this phase, and you will soon discover that salvation from low self-confidence is presenting itself to you, but you are all too muddled in your world to cure the problem. Unless a life-changing miracle happens to come your way.

Chapter 5: Ideas for Increasing Self-Confidence

Don't be duped. Even the most confident people have insecurities, and even the most competent people have flaws.

Though we may have wished to be the perfect people we see in others, we must recognize that nothing is perfect. The things we want to happen in our lives don't always happen the way we want them to, no matter how carefully we plan. The things we desire will not pass us by if we do not work toward achieving them.

However, making things happen requires effort.

And self-assurance is not something that comes naturally to people.

According to one author, the most beautiful people do not just happen.

They must experience hardship, suffering, defeat, struggle, and loss before they can truly comprehend the depth of their worth.

Everyone is wired for recognition, achievement, and celebrity. The ability to believe in oneself was not given at random; it exists in all of us. As with everything else, we are on equal footing with the person sitting next to us. The distinction is in how we treat the abilities that have been bestowed upon us.

The early development of self-confidence is rooted in our childhood, how we were raised, the opportunities that shaped us into the people we are, and our reactions to the challenges that were thrown at us.

At such a young age, We've all experienced being humiliated or encouraged. We can already give interpretations of how things happen to us at a very young age. If we failed to react positively as children for reasons such as a lack of or improper guidance, poor models, and insufficient knowledge, the subsequent stages of our lives will most likely become dependent on how things went during these ages.

However, maturity comes with age. And maturity develops as a result of our experiences. We know that experiences are among the best teachers we have. Failure to capitalize on our experiences

The encounter will only return us to the same situation until we can figure out where we went wrong.

As a result, we have no excuse for not being allowed to improve with each experience.

Increasing self-confidence is simply a matter of maturing. If you become complacent about your lack of achievement and recognition, you will fail to recognize that life is more than mediocre living.

Everyone, regardless of past experiences, can improve their self-esteem. What matters is only the present. You will be one step closer to achieving self-confidence if you take stock of yourself and believe that you can be anything and everything you want to be.

There are numerous approaches you can take to boost your self-esteem.

The keys are to dress positively that anyone can do anything and to adapt to the belief that you can be anyone and anything you set your mind to be.

If everything else fails, recall the times when you felt good because you were able to accomplish something by feeling good about yourself. As a result, you will be encouraged to become the better person you have always desired to be.

Chapter 6: What to Do When You Need to Boost Your Self-Confidence

Small differences can have a big impact. It all comes down to a single idea that will help you recreate your self-image.

Remember when you were so sure you could do something and then someone commented on how bad things went? Remember when you were struggling to complete your work satisfactorily and someone told you that you would never be promoted?

Remember when you set out to run a mile and people questioned you for doing so? Remember all of those occasions. They are all based on pessimistic commentary that served no purpose other than to destroy the positive spirit within you that says "you can."

Positive thinking is close to self-confidence.

If you think positively of yourself and consider all the positive qualities you have while considering the value of those you lack, you can at least convince yourself that you can do and make things happen.

Positive thinking does not imply being overly optimistic about something unattainable. Setting realistic goals that you can achieve without limiting your abilities is essential for boosting self-confidence and positive thinking.

When we set out to do something, we often overestimate our abilities and plan to achieve goals that are beyond our current capabilities. This, we argue, would encourage us to work more hours.

But what we fail to realize is that if we fail to meet our own and the expectations of those watching us, we will be discouraged from trying again.

You see, on our first attempts, it is preferable to set achievable goals rather than confidence-boosting-unrealistic goals that will leave us disappointed.

When you need to feel good about yourself, remember that our bodies hormonal balance is largely responsible. Thus,

You can change your mood by stimulating yourself. For example, if you have a vivid memory of being able to accomplish something, or if you once had "cheerleaders" who pushed you to achieve greater things, you can undoubtedly use them to manipulate your emotions. If not, recall times when you were pleased with yourself. Controlling your moods and emotions can help boost your overall confidence.

We've all been critics at some point in our lives. Unfair criticism not only makes us vulnerable to negative thoughts, but it also has an impact on our overall personal perspectives.

Have you ever noticed how we criticize ourselves without realizing we can't say the same things to other people? We are harsher on ourselves than we realize.

As a result, with each negative comment from this critic, we are upset and unconfident. It's like tearing down the walls we've been building for a long time in exchange for a few unjust remarks that we rarely need.

Avoid making broad statements about yourself because these are the things that will eventually rob you of your positive self-image. Recreating the comments you make to yourself will have a significant impact on your self-esteem.

In the end, destruction originates within us. Others may argue that we are influenced by outside pessimism. True, but this will only affect us once we allow ourselves in. As a result, you only need to build barriers against negative inputs while strengthening your underlying foundations.

Chapter 7: Advice to Help You in Increasing Self Confidence

Confidence is the stuff of life from which we are all made. The difference is simply our understanding and acceptance of things.

Some people are simply more interested in recognizing themselves and their abilities than others.

Everything depends on our perception of ourselves, our understanding of possibilities, and our ability to apply our understanding and perception.

We believe that, like wealth, self-confidence is something that everyone else possesses except us. Life, you see, was created equal and is meant to be equal.

Inequality stems from our perceptions of what we already have but fail to recognize, as well as what others have that we desire.

Don't be too hard on yourself. Don't deny yourself the pleasures of life. Take stock of yourself and stop making excuses like looking at your neighbor's fences while blinding your eyes to the gold mine that exists on your property.

No one can take away our beauty to save us. We were all given talents, skills, beauty, and wonder, as well as the ability to use or disregard them. However, once we recognize our potential, we will discover that there is more to life than mediocrity.

We must recognize, however, that we are constrained in a few areas.

However, these are offset by the fact that we have the potential to excel in other areas. Only we need to discover our veins and fortes.

Our understanding may be hampered by our prior experiences. However, this does not negate the fact that we can broaden our perception of ourselves if we just take one more step toward creating positive images of who we truly are. Remember that our success or failure is determined by how we carry ourselves. It does not imply that when your coworker

achieves far more, he takes these accomplishments from your vaults of potential. It simply means that he recognized his abilities and used them to his advantage.

In general, self-confidence and how we increase it are only achieved when we dare to do things that we initially thought were far beyond our abilities. We sometimes fail to recognize how simple things can help us achieve the heights of confidence.

There are numerous approaches to developing our confidence.

Activities such as improving your verbal skills through writing and public relations will significantly contribute to your sense of self-esteem. Most of us are afraid of appearing in public. However, once we overcome this fear, we are likely to discover more of our capabilities. You may also find self-confidence reinforcement by developing your natural talents.

If you enjoy combining notes and poetry, or if you have a natural inclination to become involved with music, you can help save yourself from low self-esteem by redirecting your interest to more useful activities. You could write music and allow others to appreciate your compositions, or you could get involved in poetry and develop your genius.

There are limitless possibilities; all you have to do is be open to them. Remember that the only being who can prevent you from developing is yourself, and the only being who can save you from happiness is also yourself.

Decide whether you want to be your worst enemy or your best friend.

Chapter 8: Develop Self-Belief from Within

The central issue when addressing the development of self-confidence in an individual who has long believed that his self-worth is inadequate is how to get self-confidence.

Individuals with a strong sense of self can bear themselves better than those with a weak sense of self. They are the achievers, the center of society, and the people in the spotlight. They walk straight, speak clearly, and have a subtle and obvious influence on others. In short, they are those who care, and they can be seen from afar.

Self-assured people are sometimes adored by society. However, there are those self-assured people who, simply by leaving, make the room lighter.

These are two very different displays of self-assurance. One undermines a person's credibility, while the other enhances his personality. And you do not want the consequences of being overconfident in yourself, which is that people no longer see you as effective, but rather as an annoyance in their daily lives.

Self-assurance comes from within. Outside stimulation can be beneficial, but knowing yourself and applying that knowledge to gain confidence is the key to gaining self-confidence, To gain self-confidence, you must understand that your limitations must not limit you and your characteristics must not destroy you. Instead, use all of these factors to create a personality that will benefit you and those around you.

"Know thyself!" exclaims Delphi's Oracle. Though this was said thousands of years ago, it is undeniably true that the wisdom it contains is still applicable today.

Learn about yourself and gain confidence. Recognize, however, that knowledge comes from within you. As a result, you must accept the fact that unless you accept your flaws and perfection, the demons of low self-confidence will linger in your being indefinite.

Knowing too much about yourself can be dangerous if your self-control foundations are not well developed. You would be exposed to your flaws, and because you do not yet have control, you may be eaten by your flaws.

This condition is closely related to thought rumination, in which you appear to go around in a circle of thoughts about your losses and failures regardless of your successes.

Another risk of losing control of yourself while attempting to gain self-confidence is that you may become overconfident and lose sight of the true value of having a sense of self. As previously stated, overconfidence is just as dangerous as a lack of confidence.

This would return you to failures or, worse, to eventual failure.

Knowing yourself is one factor that can be either dangerous or beneficial.

Self-awareness frequently assists people in realizing how wonderful their creation was. They learn to value their abilities and characteristics, which are as unique as those of others. We are indeed all unique.

Our distinguishing characteristics can be seen by closely examining our abilities and limitations. Our individuality is manifested in the natural gifts that contribute to our greater self-worth. Our uniqueness can be seen in our potential, which we can choose to ignore or maximize at will.

All of these are truths that you would be unaware of unless you learned to contemplate your being and become aware of who you truly are.

Disclaimer

This book was written solely for educational purposes. Every effort has been made to ensure that this book is as comprehensive and accurate as possible.

However, typographical or content errors may occur. Furthermore, the information in this book is only up to the date of publication. As a result, this book should only be used as a guide, not as the final authority. The purpose of this e-book is to teach. The author and publisher do not warrant that the information in this book is complete and are not liable for any errors or omissions.

www.ingramcontent.com/pod-product-compliance
Lightning Source LLC
LaVergne TN
LVHW050348160826
845677LV00014B/3852

9798359312493